JUST LOOK UP

JUST LOOK UP

Five Life-Saving Phrases Every
~~Kid~~ Human Needs to Hear

Joe Beckman

Minneapolis

ISBN 13: 978-1-63489-372-5

Library of Congress Catalog Number: 2020914388
Printed in the United States of America
First Printing: 2020

26 25 24 23   9 8 7 6

Cover design by Luke Bird
Interior design by Patrick Maloney

Wise Ink Creative Publishing
807 Broadway St. NE
Suite 46
Minneapolis, MN 55413

wiseink.com

This book is dedicated to the late Joani Weeres. Joani was my wife's grandmother. However, soon after I met her over twenty years ago, she became my grandmother as well. Joani's spirit of love and kindness is embedded into the fabric of every page in this book.

Joani passed away in the spring of 2020, only months before this book was completed. Although this amazing woman didn't get to see it in its finished state, I believe she's smiling down from above, beaming with pride. We love you, Joani, and we miss you so very much. Your legacy is strong and will continue to impact our family for generations to come. I promise to keep a signed copy of the book so the next time we see each other we'll have something to read. The only thing I ask in return is that you save me a polka or two so we can dance the night away.

Contents

Prologue

The idea for this book has been in my head for the past few years. An expanding business and an increasingly busy speaking schedule, not to mention a growing family, kept me from giving the project the time it needed. However, I decided in the winter of 2019 that this book needed to be a priority. I didn't know for sure how I'd fit in writing, but I knew I needed to reorganize things to make it happen. So I started. Slowly but surely, it was taking shape.

And then?

The COVID-19 pandemic began in early March 2020, as I was writing. This, of course, cleared my travel schedule completely. While physical isolation meant my days now involved homeschooling my three kids, it also meant I could give finishing this book the attention it needed.

The irony of all this is not lost on me. Writing a book

about human connection, the idea that is central to my life and work, during a time when we have been forced into isolation by a virus is certainly not a circumstance I could have predicted.

We live in a world far more uncertain than before the pandemic. However, I believe that the Five Phrases—and the central theme of human connection that is the spine of this entire book—have NEVER been, nor ever will be, more important.

Grunt!

Preface to the Second Printing

Hi friend!

Joe here. Before you go jumping into the book . . . I need to add a minor, yet important update.

Throughout you'll read about this company called Happy Caveman that Scott Kollmann and I started as we launched our message into the world. Since the time the book was written, we have "evolved" a bit.

A few months into the pandemic I was introduced to a gentleman by the name of Curt Slater. Curt was a National Distinguished Principal of the Year in 2018, and after we sat down for the first time on his rickety pontoon boat on the Mississippi River, I knew that we needed Curt to be a part of our team. Together, the three of us have formed TILL360.

TILL stands for

Teach
Inspire
Listen
Learn

360 means that we have a comprehensive, "whole community" approach and partner with schools and districts over multiple years to help support their goals and initiatives. It starts with listening and learning, and together with the school/district leadership team we form a plan around how we can best teach and inspire. Together, in partnership with schools, we're doing some really really cool things. Visit www.TILL360.com to learn more.

Thanks for taking the time to read this book! If at anytime you think . . . "I want MY school to partner with TILL360!" . . . we would love to start the conversation!

Love your face!

Joe

Introduction

Tick . . . tick . . . tick . . .

There I stood, on an empty stage, watching the second hand slowly make its way around the clock on the wall. *Tick . . . tick . . . tick . . .*

The Year: 2015

The Location: Cardinal Heights Junior High in lovely Sun Prairie, Wisconsin.

The Scene: In less than thirty seconds, 486 *(Red Bull–infused)* ninth-graders would pour into the auditorium.

My Job: Keep them engaged and listening the entire time.

Gnarly.

Before I tell you how it ended (spoiler alert: not all that great), let me take a quick step back.

My name is Joe.

I'm what you call a motivational speaker (yep, that's a real job). Since 2001, in some way, shape, or form, I have been leading character programming in schools all across the country, and sometimes even the world. In 2015, my brother-in-law and best friend, Scott Kollmann, took on the additional title of business partner when he and I stepped out on our own and cofounded Happy Caveman. Our brand's mission?

To reclaim the lost art of human connection.

Why Happy Caveman? Well, to survive, cavemen relied heavily on their community, their connection to each other. Without the group, they were susceptible to predators or starvation. They needed each other.

And how does what mattered to cavemen matter now? To boil it down as simply as possible, we need each other! There's zero doubt we are at our happiest, most content, and most purpose-led selves when, like cavemen twenty-seven thousand years ago, we are in connection with a tribe. Happy Caveman believes that, as technology continues to progress exponentially (for which we are incredibly grateful), we cannot lose the one thing that got us humans this far in the first place: human connection.

Human Connection Matters.

I live in Minneapolis with my wife, Jess, and our three kids, but most weeks, I'm in a different city and/or state than my family. I share this "human connection matters" message in schools all across the world through an engaging online curriculum and dynamic live events for students, educators, and parents. Scott manages our marketing and runs the business. Our work and reach are constantly evolving, and we're busier than ever.

But that's not *at all* how it was when we started. Which brings us back to Cardinal Heights Junior High in 2015.

I had been doing this "speaking in schools" thing for fourteen years, but for the very first time, this was a message I had developed completely on my own, without the framework of an organization behind me or talking points I knew I had to include.

This was just me, and what my gut told me these kids needed to hear.

The auditorium doors opened. The kids rushed in. And I was a hot, hot mess.

I was talking, but they were not *listening,* which meant I was *struggling.* And they were *wiggling,* and I was certain the teachers in the back were *judging,* and my face was completely *sweating.*

Then, the doors to the auditorium opened loudly. Everyone turned and looked at the back of the room. The principal walked in with one more ninth-grade student. This one had bright blue hair. She had her hood up and earbuds in, and as I tried to continue my talk I watched her slouch down in the last seat, in the last row.

Clearly, this was the last place Blue Hair Girl wanted to spend her morning.

I know what you're thinking right now. You're thinking I'm going to try to get you to read one of those sappy, feel-good books where I tell you Blue Hair Girl's whole life completely changed after hearing my stupid talk, and you're outta here.

All good. Stick around. That's not how the story ends.

In fact, if I can be honest, the talk at Cardinal Heights? It wasn't a strikeout in the bottom of the ninth with the bases loaded, but it certainly wasn't a home run either. If I had to give it a grade, I would say it was a solid C.

However, the thing I remember most about that day in Sun Prairie, Wisconsin, is what happened *after* the talk.

When the last student walked back to class, I packed up my stuff in the auditorium. On my way out of the school to my minivan, I passed through the cafeteria. I was merely feet from the main exit, bound for Minneapolis. But. Out of the corner of my eye, sitting against a bank of lockers, I spied Blue Hair Girl. But she was no longer alone—she was sitting with a group of her friends, who, funnily enough, also had blue hair. (It was a club . . . who knew?)

I had two choices.

Choice one: Go. Parking lot. Minivan. A nearly 300-mile drive to Minneapolis ahead of me.

Choice two: Stop. Have a conversation . . . no doubt an awkward conversation . . . with a student who wanted nothing to do with me in the first place.

I'm the king of awkward. There was never really any question I'd go with choice two.

I struck up a conversation with Blue Hair Girl—except it was really more of a monologue. I was talking; she was . . . not.

I tried everything:
good jokes,
bad jokes,
dad jokes.

Nothing worked.

Finally, I said, "Blue Hair Girl"—I literally called her "Blue Hair Girl"—"I have a daughter at home who's never seen hair quite as . . . blue . . . as yours. If you let me take one quick selfie—thirty seconds, tops—I'll be out of your life . . . out of your hair [*your blue, blue hair*], forever." She agreed. And even though it was subtle, I swore I caught Blue Hair Girl with the tiniest smile.

I had a four-hour drive home that day. For once, I didn't clutter my mind with the radio, a podcast, or anything else. Despite the average grade I'd given myself, and all the things I knew I'd improve for the next time I spoke to a group of students, I couldn't shake the feeling:

SHE is why I do what I do.

She may not have cared about my presentation that day, but the truth is, the reason I even have a presentation in the first place is because of students like Blue Hair Girl. The underdogs. The kids on the fringe.

Maybe it's because I'm the youngest in my family and always felt like the underdog myself, but for as long as I can remember, I've been wired to care deeply about this group. And as I've stepped out on my own and into more schools, I've realized that I'm also wired to care deeply about the athletes, and the actors, and the academic rock stars, and the artsy students. I'm wired to care deeply about teachers, and custodians, and cooks in the lunchroom. Parents, mentors, and community members? I'm wired to care deeply about them as well.

I'm wired to care deeply about *every* person who is hurting. *Everyone* who is questioning whether they— or any of this—matters. And what I've come to realize over eighteen years is that these people are *everywhere* and come from *every* walk of life.

Whether it's Minneapolis or Montana or Malaysia, fifteen-year-olds or fifty-five-year-olds, the poorest parts of a city or a rural farm in the country or a gated community in the suburbs . . . feelings of loneliness, anxiety, and disconnection are at an all-time high, while human connection is at an all-time low.

Coincidence? I think not.

The (Dis)connection Epidemic

A study published in April 2019 in the *Journal of Abnormal Psychology* reported the number of young people with mental health disorders has more than doubled over the past decade.[1]

Nearly half of all college students, many times from the most esteemed institutions, say they've been so overwhelmed by anxiety they could hardly function.

Shockingly, nearly one in three college students has seriously contemplated taking their own life.[2]

I don't know about you, but these statistics take my breath away in the worst way possible. More than ever, kids (many of whom are reading this book themselves) are feeling the burn of living in the

fast-paced,
do-it-all,
win-at-any-cost,
boredom-is-bad,

---

1   https://health.usnews.com/wellness/for-parents/articles/2019-04-22/teen-depression-is-on-the-rise

2   https://www.affordablecollegesonline.org/college-resource-center/college-student-depression/

hyperconnected-yet-totally-disconnected society we surround them with.

More than ever, they are looking for answers. Looking to their teachers, coaches, parents, youth pastors, mentors . . . anyone who's walked a little further down the path of life than they have.

And the questions they are asking are big. They're questions like:

Why am I here?
How can I feel less alone?
Am I enough?
What's the point of *any* of this?

Students, I want you to know that I hear you. I see you.

Adults, the questions I'm asking *us* to reflect on are:

What are we telling them?
How are we responding?
Is it honest?

What are the most important messages ALL kids need to hear in today's world?

The answers to all those questions are exactly what I sought to provide when I gave that talk at Cardinal Heights Junior High in Sun Prairie, Wisconsin. And although the answers I provided were not fully fleshed out or polished or all that engaging—just ask Blue Hair Girl—I felt like I was on to something.

Finally, after years of shifting, tweaking, trying, failing, and growing (lather, rinse, repeat) since that day, I think I've found a message that really moves the emotional needle . . .

Love YOU
Push Through
Just Look Up

I call these **the Three Phrases,** and they have been the backbone of my message since then. Love YOU focuses on self-worth, Push Through is about resilience, and Just Look Up is about, you guessed it, human connection.

Over the last few years, the feedback these phrases have elicited has been nothing short of breathtaking.

Since I started giving this talk regularly, I have received messages from students about how one or more of the Three Phrases has significantly impacted and, more times than I can count, *saved* their lives. Take this message, for example:

> *Hey Joe, I didn't get a chance to stick around and talk to you today, but I figured this was the next best thing. Everything you said today, I really needed to hear. Because of you I came home, went through all of my notebooks, and shredded every paper I had written I wasn't good enough on. I shredded every paper I wrote about suicide on. I got rid of the pills that I had left over from my surgery, and in the remaining pages of my notebooks I wrote down positive things and things that I remembered from your talk. I can't explain how thankful I am for everything, and I just want you to know you've done more for me than anyone else. I'll never forget it. Thank you.*

Messages like these are both humbling and motivating. It's humbling to hear that my words impact another human being on that level, and at the same time, it lights a fire inside me to continue to create more.

Shortly after I began hearing from students, I started hearing from adults too. These teachers, parents, and other humans from all walks of life generally told me one of two things: they themselves needed to hear these messages, or they wished they had heard them earlier in their lives.

By now, I hear about the impact of the Three Phrases on a weekly basis. Thus, the idea for this book was born.

My thought was that more people need this message than I can speak to in real life, and I want it available to everyone. Youth *and* adults. And because this is a book and not a speech, I have the time and space to break down two extra phrases: **Fail On** and **Yeah Toast!**

So instead of just three . . . you get five! *(virtual fist pound)*

But wait! There's more! At the end of each chapter, I've

included Caveman Wisdoms: practical tips, tools, and tactics that will help you apply the knowledge acquired from that specific chapter.

The point of this book isn't just to take five universal truths that live in your head and move them to your heart. That's not enough. If this book is going to truly move the needle, the message needs to move from your heart into your hands. Because no matter how inspirational a book like this can feel, none of it will do a bit of good unless you do something with it.

The Ultimate Hope

The bottom line for me is this: life is hard. Sometimes really hard. If we could focus our energy and intention in a few different areas, what should they be?

I feel like so many of us are looking for help with that question. I'm not here to claim I have the perfect plan, but I have thought about this extensively. And while I don't have a PhD, I do have the last eighteen years of experience, during which I've worked in over a thousand schools and connected with hundreds of thousands of students and their teachers. And I can see that what Happy Caveman is sharing and talking about really, really resonates.

The Five Phrases are what every human needs to navigate the general journey all of us will experience.

Maybe one will resonate with you. Maybe it will be two or more. Regardless, no matter what "side of life" you are on as you're reading this, I hope you'll approach this book with an open mind and an open heart. Even more importantly, if any of the phrases strike a chord with you personally, my hope is that you do something about it.

#ConnectionOn!

Joe

P.S. Oh . . . and Blue Hair Girl? My first impression of her was obviously that she was completely checked out, not listening, and not about to follow through with anything I had to say that day I showed up at her junior high. Keep reading, and I promise I'll tell you how I was wrong about all that.

CHAPTER ONE

Love YOU

Masks on a Plane

I do a lot of flying for this work. Even though I've been doing it for years now, I still think it's pretty rad.

What's not so rad is the flight attendants' preflight safety speech. If you've never had the pleasure of hearing it, let me sum it up:

"Hi, and welcome aboard Delta Flight 385 to Los Angeles. If this plane crashes, we're all going to die. In case of a sudden loss in oxygen, masks will magically fall from the sky . . ."

This may or may not be what they say. At this point, I've heard it so many times I no longer pay attention. But my summary is close, I assure you.

Then, they give a very specific instruction to the passengers fortunate enough to be flying with a small child.

"Before you assist those around you with *their* mask, put on your own mask first."

I'm certain that's what they say on this part.

But excuse me, WHAT?

That statement makes about as much sense as eating packaged ramen noodles on a daily basis, thinking they're part of a well-balanced diet.

I have three kids. If they're all flying with me, the flight attendant is telling me I'm supposed to put *my own* mask on first? How does that work?

And then it hits me. *Right.*

How could I, as a father, properly get masks on all three of my kids if I were struggling to breathe? I would be panicked, and I wouldn't work as quickly as needed to keep them all safe.

And you don't have to be a parent for this analogy to work. It applies to all of us: If you are gasping for breath, how can you possibly have the presence of mind to help someone else breathe properly?

This is where my first phrase comes in: Love YOU.

Not "I love you."
Love YOU.
Love yourself first.

Some of us have trained ourselves to ignore what we need and instead be really good at seeing all the different people in our life who need oxygen:

friends,
siblings,
family,
complete strangers.

We notice them flailing, struggling to be their best selves, and we jump in to help. We rush over and put on their masks when they're in need. We fill them up with words of encouragement. We reassure them that no matter how bad it feels at this moment, it's not always going to be this way. We find them the help they need to overcome whatever they're struggling with.

However . . .

When it comes to our own selves?
When *we're* the ones who need oxygen?
It's a completely different script, narrated by a completely different voice.

A voice filled with judgment and shame.
A voice focused on negativity and self-doubt.
A voice that constantly questions, "Am I even worthy to receive this oxygen in the first place?"

The voice of Not Enough. The NEs.

You know what I'm talking about. We all have them.

For so many of us, the NEs start right away in the morning.

You get out of bed, look in the mirror, point out any number of flaws, and say,
>   *Not pretty enough.*

And then, almost like a song stuck on repeat, it continues on throughout the day.

You make an error on the field . . .
>   *Not athletic enough.*

You get three points taken off a test . . .
> *Not smart enough.*

You don't get invited to that party . . .
> *Not popular enough.*

Day by day, these Not Enough messages pile up. One by one, they stack up on top of each other. And slowly, over days and months, and then years and decades,

our real voice,
the voice full of love and acceptance,
the voice of Enough,

receives less and less oxygen. For some of us, it becomes restricted to the point of suffocation.

Once the NEs get their foot in the door, it doesn't take long for their voice to become so loud, we can't even fully take a breath without hearing the chorus of Not Enoughs chanting in our head.

If you don't think all this negativity has an impact on how you treat yourself, or how you treat others, guess again.

The Shirt

I was eight years old when the NEs flooded in. At least, this is my first memory of them.

My family was celebrating Christmas, opening gifts at my grandma's house, when one was passed to me. Excitedly, I took it from a relative's hand. I mean, it was Christmas, and I was a kid . . . every present felt exciting.

And then, as I got ready to tear into the paper, it got quiet . . .

like "weird" quiet.

Like "they-know-something-I-don't" quiet.

I ripped open the present and noticed it was a shirt. Not thrilled to be opening clothes, but sensing everyone's anticipation, I unfolded it and took a closer look at what it was.

The front of the shirt had a cartoon character on it. He was overweight, with food all over his face and shirt, his belly hanging out the bottom. The bright green letters on top read:

Human Garbage Disposal.

And everyone in the room started laughing.

I didn't get it at first. I was only a second-grader.

But then it hit me:

"Right . . . the kid on the shirt is . . . me."

From that moment on, I became falsely convinced that my value to this world and the worth I had in myself weren't defined by who I was, but rather by what I looked like.

It started as a drizzle of Not Enoughs in elementary school—a negative thought here, a quick insult there. By the time I got into middle school, it had turned into a full-blown storm.

Slowly but surely, this NE gained momentum. It started to consume my life. As if my inner thoughts about my weight weren't enough, they were fueled by jesting comments from people around me. I got called "butterball," "bubble butt," and a host of other humiliating names by classmates, family, and even coaches.

Not surprisingly, it began to impact
what I wore, and what I would *never* wear.
what I ate, and what I would *never* eat.
where I would go, and where I would *never* go.

Let's just say pool parties, beaches, or any other places that required me to take my shirt off were a hard *no!*

I began to hate myself. And I'm not using that word lightly. When I looked in the mirror, I literally hated the human that looked back at me. The NE voice was loud, and it was constant, and I believed it.

By the time I got to ninth grade, I was fully convinced that the only way I was going to shake this feeling of unworthiness and feel any sort of happiness was to lose a significant amount of weight.

I severely restricted my diet.
I memorized calorie counts on all the foods I ate.
I exercised obsessively.

And although I lost a few pounds, it never seemed to be enough.

One night I remember feeling so much anger and hate, I thought, *Joe, do whatever it takes.*

That night was the first time, but certainly not the last, I made myself throw up to satisfy that voice.

I remember the carpet under my feet as I walked up the stairs to my bathroom. I remember the *click* sound as I locked the door. Worst of all, I remember the voices in my head screaming, "*Not enough, not enough, not enough,*" as I put my fingers down my throat.

And over the next few months I continued to repeat these same actions . . . a lot.

I would eat, and then I would throw up.
I would eat, and then I would throw up.
I would eat, and then I would throw up.

And even though I lost more weight, I was completely miserable.

Convincing Liars

I'm forty-one years old, and I've done a lot of work to undo the NE that lodged itself in my brain at eight years old. And yet, sometimes, I *still* disapprove of the reflection I see in the mirror.

Logically, I know now that those thoughts all through growing up were way off base: the list of things I wanted had nothing to do with my weight, and everything to do with the voice in my head that tried to keep me small and steal my confidence.

But at fourteen? Logic wasn't a big part of my life strategy. I couldn't think through undoing that disapproval of myself.

The voices kept telling me that my value and worth were defined by how much I weighed.

And like so many, I got tricked into falling for them.

You see, the thing about the NEs is that they're liars . . . really, really convincing liars. They tell us if we . . .

just lose *one* pound,
achieve this *one* grade,

receive this *one* promotion,
drive this *one* car,
or get invited to this *one* party,

<u>then</u> we will be enough. *Then* life will suddenly get so much better.

And because our original voice has been suffocated, we fully believe the new voices, full of lies, that have pushed their way in.

I meet so many people who have bought into these lies, and they're miserable. It changes not only who they are, but also how they treat others.

The Voices of Not Enough

For some, the NEs come from ***not feeling popular*** enough. They tear others down or post hurtful things to social media to feel accepted and advance their social standing.

For others, the NEs are about their appearance. They ***don't feel pretty*** enough, so they cake on a ton of makeup, or criticize someone else's appearance, or use so many filters when they post a picture that you can barely even tell they're real.

Others **don't feel loved** enough, and they go further sexually than they're really comfortable with, thinking THAT will fill the void.

Others **don't feel like they're good enough**, so they cut themselves, or drink too much, or contemplate taking every pill in the bottle to try to numb away the pain their NEs are causing.

Here's the thing: those "solutions" might make them feel better for about a minute.

They *might*.

However, with that "might" comes damage to relationships, damage to health, and damage to their self-image. Not to mention this pesky little truth: the whole thing repeats itself as soon as the high or the numbness wears away, because none of these are an actual solution.

Listen: as long as the NE voices are running the script, they will never let you feel worthy of anything.

Enough Just Because

Let me speak some truth to the NE voice in your head. The one that repeatedly says you'll be happy and fulfilled only after you _____ (fill in the blank with your own personal NE).

YOU'RE LOOKING IN THE WRONG PLACE!

You're never going to feel like you're enough *because* you're pretty, or popular, or perfect (which, news flash, is not even a thing humans can be).

Getting a lot of likes on an Instagram post?
Being the star athlete?
Giving the valedictorian speech?

Or, if you're by chance a few years older . . .

Sitting in the corner office with a fancy job title?
Owning a shiny, new luxury car?
Being in a relationship others envy?

They may be nice accomplishments, and you may have even worked hard for them. But those will never make you enough, either.

Just like passing go and collecting $200 in Monopoly, your worth isn't something you earn. It's yours for free. All you gotta do is play the game.

I meet *a lot* of people who spend *a lot* of time hustling really, really hard to figure out how they can gain worth from others.

But what I'm saying is worth . . . YOUR worth . . . is something you already have! You're enough, and you're worthy, simply *because*.

Because you're you.
Because you're here.

That's it. That's the whole truth.

Before you go on, take a deep breath
and let that sink into the deepest parts of your bones.
You're worthy, and you're enough, because you're you.

A Quiet Whisper

So maybe now you're thinking, "OK, great. I get it! I'm enough. I really am.

"But . . . how? How can I banish the NE voice from my head forever, so I have the confidence to live like someone who knows they're enough?"

Here's how:

**Stop trying so damn hard
to completely banish that voice.**

Wait, what?! That doesn't make any sense.

Hear me out.

The unfortunate truth is some NEs may never go away entirely. Although they may not be as loud as they once were, they'll remain a whisper, because like it or not, they're deeply rooted in who we are.

If the goal becomes lowering the volume of the loud NE voice to a whisper, accepting that the whisper may stick around instead of banishing it, we reduce the power that NE has over us. Significantly. That acceptance gives life and oxygen back to our real voice.

Make no mistake about it: taking ownership of our NEs, instead of the NEs having ownership over us, is the equivalent of putting on our own oxygen mask. When we dismantle our own NEs, we can truly help others quiet or banish theirs.

My NE about my weight is the perfect example of this.

My weight was an intensely painful part of my childhood. That particular NE ran my life for many years, until I was able to understand it was a lie. Has it completely gone away?

Nope.

However, now that I'm an adult, it's no longer screaming at me, no longer constantly controlling every move I make. It's more of a quiet whisper, one I really don't hear too often anymore.

Today, because I did a lot of work to dismantle my own NE, I spend a lot less time trying to think of ways to convince others *I am* worthy, and a lot more time helping others see *they are* worthy. The oxygen I give to myself by owning my NE allows me to amplify the amount of oxygen I'm able to give to others.

And ultimately, I'm convinced *THIS* is the reason we are here:

to somehow,
in some way,
put on someone else's oxygen mask,
and help them breathe a little bit easier.

Maybe you're going to do something huge with public attention that will help millions, or maybe you're going to quietly be an amazing friend who helps make life better for one other person.

Make no mistake about it. You are here to do something, for someone.

However, don't forget that flight attendant's advice. The best way to help someone else breathe is to make sure we're breathing properly first.

By taking ownership of those Not Enough voices, quieting them instead of trying to eliminate them, you take back control. That control, in turn, provides your brain some oxygen. That oxygen allows you to breathe properly, which allows you to help others breathe properly.

Friends, Phrase #1 is the foundation ALL this is built on.

Love YOU.

Caveman Wisdoms: Love YOU

It's easy to constantly tell yourself, "I'm not enough."

Oftentimes, because it's so deeply rooted in us, we do it unconsciously. This can make it a very short path from "just fine" to "stuck in a rut" to "self-hate/self-harm." I get it because I've been there.

Simply put, though, if you are feeling these things, your NE voice is too loud, and it needs to be tamed. Is it easy? No. In fact, it might be some of the most difficult work you'll ever do. Is it important? Yes, 100 percent! We get a small window to make an impact in this world. The sooner we get these NEs tamed, the sooner our impact can be felt.

Below are three steps to help change the way you see yourself and put Phrase #1, "Love YOU," into action.

Step 1: Stop comparing.

Yes, I know. This is way, WAY easier said than done. Stay with me here—we're going to break it into steps.

Listen, you may never have what "they" have. Yep . . . the proverbial "they" may always seem prettier/ stronger/smarter/funnier. It may never feel fair to you to not have what you think they do.

Remember, though: you almost never have the whole picture of what someone else's life is really like. You're nearly always comparing yourself to your perception of what they have, or the carefully curated version of themselves they let you see.

You could play this comparison game for the rest of your life if you're not aware you're doing it. So, what can you do about it?

The key here is to notice what this looks like in your life. Where does comparison creep in? When is the NE voice the loudest? When do you notice yourself feeling insecure?

When you make yourself aware of the things that trigger the NE voice, you can come up with ways to pivot in order to help you stop.

For instance: if scrolling through Instagram for fifteen minutes straight makes you feel jealous and unworthy, recognize that for what it is. Acknowledge your NE voice is talking to you, then move on to something else.

Or, if you have a physical attribute that you can't stand, whether it's permanent like a birthmark or changeable like my weight, acknowledge that you hear it, remind yourself that you're not defined by it, and focus on one thing that you can do for others in order to get out of your own head.

Noticing when your NE voice is the loudest, and acknowledging that you're playing the comparison game, is the first step.

Step 2: Counteract the NEs.

The next step is changing the way you talk to yourself. When you catch yourself in the moment of comparison, what can you say or do to counteract it?

In the Instagram example, maybe it's simply closing the app, signaling to your NE voice that you're not listening. Or maybe, if it's a bigger problem, it's muting that person in your feed or deleting the app altogether.

What do you need to do to make the NE voice quieter?

The goal here is to stop focusing on all the things you think you're not and start focusing on all the things you are and could be. Because make no mistake about it, YOU bring something to the table equally as valuable as anything anyone else can bring. You may not be able to see it right now, but it's true.

One other option on this step is this: consider being brave and confiding in one friend about a specific NE you have and what you're trying to do to make it stop. Have him or her hold you accountable for following through on what you need to do. Do the same for your friend.

You are definitely not alone in dealing with NE voices. Having just one person to help you be accountable to your commitment can really make a difference.

Step 3: Change the script.

It's one thing to work to counteract your specific NEs. It's another to actively work to build yourself up in general.

My "Change the Script Challenge" is simple and straightforward. I dare you to take it! It's five easy steps, and it takes about one whole minute.

1. Find a Post-it Note.

2. Get a Sharpie.

3. Write down these three words: *You. Are. Enough.*

4. Put this message somewhere you'll see it regularly, like your bathroom mirror.

5. Read it. Out loud. Every day.
   Especially the days that hurt the most.

It's not magic. It won't wipe away every NE forever, and it won't completely prevent them from coming back. But it's a great practice. Besides, not only has positive self-talk been shown to improve the way you look at yourself, but research also suggests it lowers rates of depression, helps you build coping skills, and even has an impact on your physical health.[3]

---

3   https://www.mayoclinic.org/healthy-lifestyle/stress-management/in-depth/positive-thinking/art-20043950

Positive self-talk is a way to put on your own oxygen mask first, realizing that you have to take care of yourself in order to best help others.

And that's truly the hope of these three steps: finding simple ways we can be good to ourselves. Simple ways we can put our own mask on first. Because we know that the NEs are going to be loud, prevalent, and relentless. It's just who they are, and it's just what they do.

Again, the point isn't to banish them completely, but rather to get them down to a quiet whisper.

These "my-mask-first" steps help us do just that.

CHAPTER TWO

Push Through

Friday Night Lights

I grew up in a suburb of St. Paul, Minnesota, the youngest of three kids from what is fair to say was a sports-minded family. And although we loved all our hometown teams (Vikings, Gophers, North Stars), it was the Minnesota Twins baseball team that created the strongest bond between us. In fact, in 1985, we took a family vacation to Florida to see the Twins in spring training. We were able to meet nearly every player, including my favorite Twin of all time, Kirby Puckett.

Sports were our jam.

From the time I was very little, it was football in the fall, basketball in the winter, baseball in the spring and summer.

My siblings played, my dad coached, and my mom supported it all with the driving and the laundry and the meals-on-the-go and the cheering. We were all in on sports in the Beckman family. And when we weren't playing on official teams, we were out with neighborhood friends, playing pickup games of everything from street hockey to kick the can to capture the flag . . . ANYTHING that involved a win or a loss.

It was sports. All. Day. Long.

Truth be told, despite the NEs in my head, I was a pretty good athlete. This was not because I was extremely gifted, but rather because as the youngest, if I wanted to play with my older siblings, sports were what I did all day. If you practice anything practically from birth, you're going to be decent at worst.

I literally used to dream about playing pro baseball. I would lie awake at night imagining what my name would sound like when called by the announcer, or what it would be like to make a game-saving catch (like my hero Kirby did in Game Six of the 1991 World Series) or hit the game-winning home run in the bottom of the ninth (like Kirby did only one half-inning later).

I was mildly confident in my abilities early on, but it wasn't until I was crowned "Home Run King" in fourth grade, and given an obscenely large trophy as my reward, that I became utterly convinced I was going to get there one day.

I was lucky enough to be near the top of my class by junior high, and I had big aspirations of that trend continuing through high school. I chose St. Thomas Academy, an all-male military high school known for discipline in the classroom (which I needed) and dominance in sports (which I loved). This was going to be a perfect fit for me.

I was particularly excited to play varsity football. St. Thomas had been a powerhouse in our state for many decades, and I knew the teammates who would become like brothers for the next four years would be of state championship lineage and caliber. And for this kid, a state championship victory was the ultimate prize.

Of course, the NE voice would still creep in, making me aware of how my uniform fit or telling me I wasn't good enough. However, my innate competitive nature, my love for my teammates, and the shared goals we all had helped to quiet that voice. I really enjoyed being an athlete. I liked my teammates, and I felt a sense of accomplishment and identity. Sports made me feel worthy.

Sports were my life. And life was good.

So let me ask you a question:
What's the one thing you love more than anything else?

Maybe it's

a sport or a hobby,
gaming with friends,
or science or math or writing,

or, if you're super weird: running. Where my cross-country people at? You run for fun . . . which is weird for those of us who don't.

Imagine the one thing you love doing more than anything in the world. The activity that gets you fired up just by thinking about it. The one where time becomes nonexistent; where two hours feel like two minutes.

And now imagine that one thing being taken away.

Fractured

It seemed like the pain came out of nowhere.

I remember waking up one morning the summer between eighth and ninth grades with searing pains in my lower back. At first, I tried to ignore them, hoping they might just magically go away. But they didn't do that—in fact, they got worse.

I avoided telling my parents because I was afraid that I would miss a practice, or even a game. However, when the pain became constant, it started impacting not only my play on the field, but also how I treated people off the field. I was becoming irritable, angry, and bitter. I remember even praying to God, begging him to make this go away. But it didn't, and eventually it became obvious to everyone around me that I needed to have this checked out.

So a few weeks later, I got an MRI.
A few days later, I received the news.
A few seconds later, I was completely crushed.

"Joe," the doctor began cautiously, "you can see here you have a stress fracture in your lower back."

"What does that mean?" I asked.

The doctor continued, "It means you can't play contact sports until it heals. No basketball, and certainly no football."

Fourteen-year-old me quickly tried to make sense of this. "Gotcha. So what are we talking about here? A few weeks? A month?"

Dr. Bad News sighed and went on. "No, Joe. I don't think you understand. It's going to be at least two years. In fact, there's a chance you won't be able to play again."

Wait . . . *what?*

The doctor explained how serious this injury was— the long-term impact of not letting it heal completely could lead to permanent damage that could complicate things for the rest of my life. With that news out in the open, he explained the treatment. I was going to need to wear a large brace that would extend from my chest to my waist and wrap around my back.

"Let's just say you're not going to move all that . . .

briskly. In fact, for the next two years, you're going to look and feel a bit robotic."

If I told you that I was close to turning Dr. Bad News into Dr. Bloody Nose, would you judge me?

After the doctor left, I sat in the office with my dad, both of us stunned. I had just chosen a high school based on making competitive sports a central part of my experience. I hadn't even been a St. Thomas Academy cadet for a single day, and it already looked like I'd never put on that blue and white uniform.

The thing I was best at,
the thing I was known for,
the thing that made the NE voice not nearly so loud,
my entire identity until this point in my life, was . . .

Sports.

And sports were GONE.

Low vs. Grow

Life has a funny way of punching us in the mouth.

For some of us, it happens early.
For others, it's later.
For some, it happens more often than for others.
But make no mistake, all of us are going to feel that punch at some point.

Maybe for you, like me, it was an injury or a disability, and it changed what you could do.

Maybe you're the kid who has been bullied incessantly since second grade.

Maybe you know exactly what it feels like to have parents who fight. A lot.

Maybe you've lost someone really close to you, in a way you didn't see coming.

The truth is, many of you have dealt with things no human should ever have to experience. For some of you, it happened when you were a kid, and for others, it's happening now.

And it sucks.
And it hurts.

And it's unfair.
And I'm sorry.

If you're anything like I was, you might be asking,
Why me?
What did I do to deserve this?
How can I possibly make it through?

It's what I call "living in the low."

For a year after I received the news, I was right there
. . . low.

On the outside, I was great at putting on a mask and
acting as if everything were fine. I was already hiding
the NE; now I took pretending it was fine that sports
were out of my life and added that to my list of masks.
But on the inside, I was

Angry
Hurt
Sad
Frustrated

I would ask . . .

Why me?
Why Me?
WHY ME?

And the truth is ALL of that . . . is completely normal.

Listen, when life punches you in the mouth, it's **normal** to

have *TONS* of questions
be *INCREDIBLY* angry
feel *ALL* that pain
be *COMPLETELY* numb.

It's normal to feel any or all of that. But at some point—and I can't say for sure how long that will be for you because the truth is, it's different for everybody—you're going to get sick and tired of feeling angry and low. At some point, the fog will start to lift. If you're like me, you're going to get this tug on your heart that says,

"THIS ISN'T HOW LIFE IS MEANT TO BE LIVED!"

And when that opportunity presents itself, I urge you to seize it. Make the choice right then and there to transcend from "living in the low" to "finding a way to grow."

The Audition

For me, the fog lifted about a year after the diagnosis of my stress fracture.

I was a sophomore, sitting in my second-hour English class, when a woman by the name of Wendy Short-Hayes walked into the classroom. She was the theater director, and she was there to recruit actors to try out for the upcoming fall musical, Studs Terkel's *Working*.

Remember: I went to an all-male military academy. Let's just say participation in the fine arts was lacking.

I was only kind of paying attention as she talked about how there were these great roles, how everyone who's ever tried theater says they *"loved theater!"* and how it was a chance to try something new.

Then, she said something that really got my attention.

Playing to her audience, she said, "You get to come down to Visitation [the all-girls school!] every day for rehearsal . . ."

Oh, hey. **Now** I was listening.

One voice in my head said, *"You've always kind of wanted to do something like this, and you've never really had the chance because of sports. . ."*

Another voice, equally loud, yelled, *"Shut your face! You would be doing this for the wrong reasons. You're going to fail! Your friends are going to laugh at you. Your parents are going to disown you. You're an athlete, not an actor!"*

For the rest of my classes that day, the only thing I could think about was the audition. When the final bell rang, I walked to the T at the end of the hallway.

Go right: head to my bus.
Go left: audition for this play.

Eyes closed . . . heart pounding . . . knees shaking,

I went left.

Out the door . . . down the road . . . into the all-girls school.

I walked, terrified, into the lobby area of the auditorium. Seeing the others, I tried to blend in (which meant flirt with the girls) by making small talk, but I felt like it was obvious to everyone there that I had never done anything quite like this before.

The audition process consisted of each student walking in individually, introducing themselves, and reading an excerpt from the play. When it was my turn, my insides started rumbling, and I remember thinking, "Oh! *This* is what it feels like to get 'pee-your-pants' nervous." After I awkwardly stumbled my way into the theater and onto the stage, I introduced myself and read the excerpt that was given to us in the lobby. When I finished reading, I began walking quickly toward the exit doors. I was ready for my insides to stop talking, and for my nerves to be relieved.

And that's when I heard Wendy say, "Wow, Joe, that was really great!"

"It was?" I asked in disbelief.

"Absolutely! It was awesome! Now . . . what's your song?"

"Song?" I looked at her with wide eyes, stunned.

"Yes. This is a musical. We need to hear everyone sing. What song did you prepare?"

Whoa, whoa, whoa! I never heard about a song! Song!! SONG??

"It's OK if you don't have anything prepared. Just sing the first song that comes to your mind!"

So, I walked back onto the stage, planted my feet, looked directly into Wendy's eyes, and belted out the first song that came into my head. And that, my friends, is how I wound up singing the *Sesame Street* theme song for my very first audition.

Days later, the cast list was posted, and I ran to the theater just in case my name had somehow made it onto that sheet. There it was. Fourth from the top.

"Joe Beckman."

And then I saw it again, and then again one more time. Because of how the play was written, all the cast members played several different roles, and as I reviewed all the names/roles on the list, I learned that I was

the Mason
the College Student
and the Gas Man (seriously . . . how did she know?)

I remember the moment I stepped onto the stage at the very first rehearsal. Everything felt incredibly right. It was like I got this confirmation in my soul that ultimately, I wasn't put on this planet to be on a field, or a court, or a baseball diamond. I was, and am, meant to be on a stage.

In fact, two years later, after my back finally healed the summer before my junior year, I was at a crossroads: rejoin the football team, or stick with theater? There was no way to do both, and so . . . I stuck with theater.

I did so all the way through high school, playing a role in eight productions including *Godspell*, *Into the Woods*, and *West Side Story*. Theater became the obvious choice for my major in college, and I firmly believe in my heart of hearts there is no chance I would be speaking in schools and at educational conferences, or be writing *this* book, if I hadn't suffered that injury.

Yes, pain can close doors and put an end to dreams. That part is difficult, and while you're in it, it can seem like it will never end. If this is where you are, I see you, and I know this is hard.

I know there are days when none of it makes sense, days when you question whether or not you have the strength to keep going for even one more moment.[4]

But I also want you to know this: pain can truly open doors and reveal a new set of dreams.

Pain ended up being one of my greatest teachers. The same is possible for you.

Pushing Through

Here's the thing . . .

---

4 *Hint: You do!*

I think it helps to view life's most difficult experiences—the ones that make zero sense, the ones that bring us the most pain—as a test.

Tests aren't necessarily easy or fun. They are just meant for you to finish, to get through. And when they're completed, they are something you can move forward from.

Tests also give us the opportunity to step back and ask ourselves who we really are. Tests strip away false identities we've poured ourselves into, and they show us that we're more than the painful experience we're going through. Tests root us in our authentic selves; they help reveal to us who we really are, and they often show us a resilience we didn't know we had.

And while a test likely ranks somewhere on the scale between unpleasant and excruciating, getting to the other side is a relief, and that's where the lessons are. Making it through one test lets you know you are capable of surviving the experience. Then, when the next test comes along—and I'm sorry to be the bearer of bad news, but there will absolutely be a next time—you can tell yourself, "Hey, I've done hard things before, and I can do them again."

That resilience you're creating while you're in the test gives you perspective to use for the rest of your life.

So . . .
if we don't quit,
if we push through,
if we pass this test,

the reward and the perspective we will gain are likely greater than we ever could have imagined.

You Just Need to Pass

Over the last eighteen years, I've spoken in over a thousand schools, and have shared our message of human connection with over one million students, parents, and teachers throughout the world.

I receive messages from teachers saying, "I rediscovered my purpose!" Messages from parents saying, "For the first time, my kid came home excited to tell me about their day!" Messages from students saying, "Your talk saved my life."

I love all these messages, and the ones that say things like the last example are mind-blowing. Sometimes it's hard to believe that this is where my journey has led.

But please hear me loud and clear when I say: NONE of it would have happened if I hadn't suffered, and found a way past, that injury.

Listen . . . you may be going through some heavy stuff right now. Some of you may be smack-dab in the middle of the biggest challenge of your life. Some of it may one day seem small, and some of it may cause pain forever.

Remember: try to look at these experiences as a test. A test you don't even have to ace—just pass!

Because if you can pass this test . . .
If you don't quit . . .
There's an excellent chance that on the other side of this challenge lies a better set of opportunities you would have *never seen* if life hadn't punched you in the face.

Believing that there is life on the other side of this test, and being curious about what that looks like, are the essential steps we need to take in order to recruit the courage to pursue new opportunities that are waiting for us to discover them.

But you have to make up your mind right now:

- Understand the hand you've been dealt is not the hand you'll always be playing.

- Embrace the idea that "Now what?" is a much more empowering question than "Why me?"

- Realize that while you may not have had a say in the first few chapters of your story, you, and only you, are the author of the chapters to come.

Listen, your reaction to life's big challenges and the mindset that you choose to tackle them with are on you. That may not feel fair, but it's true.

Which brings us to the second lifesaving phrase every human needs to hear: Push Through.

Caveman Wisdoms: Push Through

I don't know your story. I don't know what has punched you in the mouth, what you're trying to move past, what test you have before you.

Regardless of how big or small it is, here are a couple of key ideas to help you push through.

1. Perspective is key.

See your test or roadblock as it is, but not worse than it is. Don't sugarcoat it or put on a fake happy face, but don't catastrophize either. Being able to grow and move past it depends on your being able to see it for what it really is. Try to put the test in its appropriate place.

2. Find support.

Don't keep whatever you're experiencing to yourself . . . we are meant to be in relationship with other people. It's how cavemen survived!

Research shows time and again that strong, positive relationships (not necessarily romantic ones) have a real impact on our physical health and emotional well-being. There's even evidence that a strong relationship helps your body produce less cortisol, the hormone responsible for stress! Having even one person to talk openly with can be a real benefit to anyone.[5]

While Dr. Bad News certainly wanted what was best for me, he wasn't the one supporting me through the trial of a stress fracture. But my theater director, Wendy? She was always encouraging me, always helping me put my experience in perspective.

3. Think about what's next.

You might be in limbo for a while, not knowing what will happen next (which may be comfortable or very uncomfortable, depending on your personality). But thinking about what possibilities exist after this test can help you take the next small step in the right direction, and then the next small step after that one. Often, when we focus on just doing the next right thing, we find ourselves on the other side of the test without realizing we've made it there.

The other side may not look like a parade and fireworks . . . it may be a quiet realization that the small steps, one after the other, got us through.

---

5   https://www.nm.org/healthbeat/healthy-tips/5-benefits-of-healthy-relationships

And when you're on the other side?

First, be intentional about reflecting on the test you made it through. What steps did you take? How did your life change because of all this? Second, intentionally be on the lookout for the opportunities that revealed themselves when life didn't go how you planned. Listen, observe, ask questions . . . what opportunities showed up now that things are different than you thought they'd be?

There is life on the other side of the test. Push Through.

An important note: If you or someone you know is suffering from something bigger than you can handle on your own, please turn to professionals to guide you through it. Resources and experts exist for this very reason. We've listed some here that may be of help to you:

National Suicide Prevention Lifeline: 1.800.273.8255

Crisis Text Line: Text HOME to 741741 to connect to a crisis counselor

National Child Abuse Hotline: 1.800.422.4453

RAINN (Rape, Abuse, and Incest National
Network): 1.800.656.4673

National Eating Disorders Association Helpline:
1.800.931.2237

To Write Love on Her Arms, a nonprofit dedicated
to presenting hope and finding help for people struggling with depression, addiction, eating disorders,
self-injury, and suicide: www.twloha.com

CHAPTER THREE

Just Look Up

A Rude Awakening

On the very day I was born, one of the most preposterous moments of my life occurred.

I remember it like it was yesterday . . . I kid.

The date was April 10, 1979.
Location: St. Joseph's Hospital in St. Paul, MN.

I'm told it was a pretty typical labor and delivery for the time. After I was born and met my mom and the nurses poked and prodded at me a bit, they took me away to the nursery to give her a chance to start her recovery.

My mom recalls that as the nurse walked away with me, she said, "Kathie, take this time to rest and relax."

And that's when the really preposterous thing happened.

My mom, a wily veteran of this whole process, having already given birth twice before, took out a Tareyton cigarette and lit it up. A long exhalation of smoke came from her mouth and nose.

The nurse holding me said, "Let me know if you need an empty ashtray," as she smiled and walked out of the room.

Addicted

When I'm speaking in schools and tell young people that less than thirty years ago you could smoke a cigarette not only on an airplane, but also in a hospital, they lose their minds.

Their first response is always a question: "WHAT?"

Their second response is denial: "No way!"

Their third response is confusion: "Why?"

Pretty logical responses if you ask me.

Let's think about it. How could they allow something so bad for us to become so normal?

Were they bad doctors? No.
Bad nurses? No.
Bad patients? No.

It's simple. The answer is they didn't know what they didn't know.

They didn't know the level of addiction that resulted from smoking, and they didn't know nicotine caused cancer at exceedingly high rates. And quite frankly, they didn't really care to find out.

All they knew was it felt really, really good to smoke. So good, in fact, that even when the science started to finally show the damage smoking was doing, a large percentage of the population still didn't quit.

Maybe a more accurate way to say it is they *couldn't* quit.

They were addicted.

And today, all these years later, it's easy and popular

to wag our fingers, shake our heads, and scoff at their ignorance.

How could they not have known?
How could they have been so blind?
Why did it take so long to figure this out?

The answer, of course, is obvious. When you become addicted to something—even something you know produces negative, life-altering consequences—it's really, really, REALLY hard to beat.

Even today, with cigarette box labels that predict death with usage, all the indisputable evidence of the damage cigarettes cause, and the billions of dollars we've poured into prevention, it's not like smoking is gone.

Addiction is powerful. Always has been. Always will be.

And although it's easy for us to criticize the choices people made thirty years ago, I can't help but wonder what our kids are going to be saying about us thirty years from now.

"You gave an eight-year-old kid an iPad for eight hours a day, and you didn't worry at all about the impact?"

Hmmm . . . something tells me that's going to sound about as silly as smoking a cigarette in a hospital.

The New Addiction

As I look around today, it's becoming tragically clear this generation will have its own addiction to push through. An addiction that I fear is more powerful and just as damaging to our overall health in the long term.

The new cigarette?

Our screens.

In a study released in November 2019, phone insurance company Asurion revealed the average American looks down at their screen every ten minutes.[6]

That's ninety-six times . . . every day!

---

6   https://www.prnewswire.com/news-releases/americans-check-their-phones-96-times-a-day-300962643.html

The average teen spends over 7.5 hours a day on screens merely for entertainment's sake. Add on the 2.5 hours of screen time spent daily on education, and now they're close to ten full hours looking into a screen . . . every day!

Federal prisoners literally get twice as much outdoor time, breathing fresh air, than half of children world-wide . . . every day!

The stats are alarming.

I am addicted.
You are addicted.
Our kids are addicted.
Your grandma's addicted.

And it's only getting worse.

Phones and apps and the lighting of the screen . . . they've all been cleverly designed to hook us in and then keep us there for as long as humanly possible.[7]

That Asurion study also showed that the ninety-six times a day was a 20 percent increase over the two

---

7   https://www.wired.com/story/phone-addiction-formula/

years since they'd last conducted the same study. Now, I'm no scientist, but it's pretty easy to infer from this research that these numbers are going to continue to rise. Before we know it, 96 times a day is going to turn into 119 times a day, which of course will turn into 201 times a day. And the 201 will turn into 323 times a day and so on.

With all that looking down, it's no wonder so many people feel so disconnected. And we know that those feelings of disconnection have both physical and emotional effects.

Author and professor Brené Brown says, "Love and belonging is an irresistible need of all people. We are biologically, cognitively, physically, and spiritually wired to love, to be loved, and to belong. When those needs are not met, we don't function as we were meant to. We break. We fall apart. We numb. We ache. We hurt others. We get sick."[8]

Make no mistake about it, every minute we spend looking down is another minute we could help

---

8   https://www.psychologytoday.com/us/blog/feeling-it/201208/connect-thrive

quench that "irresistible need" for the love, belonging, and connection that all of us crave.

Human connection matters. And I'm not just saying that because it looks nice on a bumper sticker. It's true.

In fact, the most comprehensive, longitudinal study on happiness—a study by Harvard researchers that is now in its eighty-second year—proves beyond a shadow of a doubt that we are both significantly happier and healthier when we have authentic human connection present in our lives.[9]

Teachers see increased rates of engagement in their students when they shake their hands at the door. [10]

Businesses have happier and more productive employees when their boss learns their kids' first names.[11] Neighborhoods have reduced social anxiety and stress when they plan monthly happy hours.[12]

---

9 https://apnews.com/6dab1e79c34e4514af8d184d951f5733
10 https://plushcare.com/blog/advantages-of-human-touch-hugs/
11 https://www.theguardian.com/money/2006/feb/25/careers.work
12 https://www.canr.msu.edu/resources/building_neighborhood_communities_an_introduction_to_successful_neighboring

In nearly every aspect of our lives, we are better when we're together.

Human connection is like a vitamin: it improves every part of your health and well-being. The sad truth is that a lot of us are forgetting to take our vitamins.

The Age of Disconnection

Whether it's at home with families, at a restaurant with friends, or on the street with strangers, we've stopped seeing each other.

And before you protest: I know. I get it. Phones are awesome. It's true.

There's never been a tool in the history of human kind that has connected us more, occupied more of our downtime, or made our lives more efficient than a smartphone. If you've ever needed to be picked up at an airport, you know that cell phones are awesome.

Your phone holds an incredible amount of your work, school, and social life. Not being consumed by that awesomeness, however, is hard. Really hard.

What's difficult to comprehend is that in this time of connection, with this tool that makes reaching out so easy, we've never felt more alone. Our phones simply give us the *illusion* of connection. But,

real connection . . .
authentic connection . . .
the face-to-face kind of connection that requires sight, sound, smell, and (maybe most importantly) touch . . .

can never be accomplished through a screen. It just can't. And that's not just my gut feeling; there's science (and lots of it!) to prove it.

As this book is being written, nearly EVERY study conducted on the impact of smartphones on youth—specifically the impact of social media apps—tells us there is a direct correlation between our addiction to screens and the spike in mental health–related issues.[13]

Now, is lack of human connection the *only* problem? Of course not.

---

13   Twenge, Dr. Jean. *iGen: Why Today's Super-Connected Kids Are Growing Up Less Rebellious, More Tolerant, Less Happy—and Completely Unprepared for Adulthood—and What That Means for the Rest of Us*

However, that lack, caused in large part by addiction to our screens and the false sense of community they provide, is contributing significantly to higher rates of depression, self-harm, suicide, and a host of other issues.

Just like our addiction to cigarettes, there are consequences, some of them probably yet unknown, to our "look-down" culture. And these consequences are being felt everywhere, and by everyone.

I can almost guarantee there is someone in your life, maybe even someone closer than you would ever imagine, who knows exactly the feelings of loneliness and despair I'm talking about.

Oftentimes, it's a person we would never expect.

Sam

One day, after I spoke at a high school in the rural Midwest, a group of upperclassmen approached me for a picture. Based on the jackets they were wearing, it was obvious they were athletes. Since I was an athlete, I have a special affinity for groups like this, and I found small talk with the guys pretty easy.

I noticed, however, that one boy had a different de- meanor. When I asked him his name, he told me it was Sam. The way he said it confirmed my intuition. Sam, for some reason, was hurting.

"You need a few minutes alone, homie?" I asked, forcing him to make eye contact and pointing to the gym doors that led out to the hallway. He reluctantly agreed, and with his friends out of range, I said in a matter-of-fact voice, "Tell me what's going on."

Sam shared with me that the pressures of high school were starting to become overwhelming. He didn't feel like he could tell anyone, and he had very serious thoughts about ending it all.

"I just feel . . . alone," he said, through tears.

I shared some words of encouragement, gave him a bro-hug, and assured him that I was going to do my best to get him the help he needed.

When we walked back in, I found the principal and let him know I needed to talk. He took out a small notebook and asked me what was wrong.

I recapped my conversation, and I told him I felt this student needed to talk to someone right away.

The principal, still looking down, finally asked me the name of the student we were talking about. When I said "Sam," he immediately stopped writing and looked up at me, perplexed.

"We only have one Sam in the whole school. You don't mean . . . *Sam?*" His disbelief was obvious.

"Yeah . . . bigger guy," I said.

"Oh no," he said as he grasped the enormity of the situation. "Sam's the quarterback of our varsity football team."

The principal wasn't in disbelief because Sam's role as quarterback made him more important than any other student at the school. However, his astonishment spoke to how unexpected it was for this news to be about the kind of kid who seemed like he had it all. How could Sam possibly be depressed, even suicidal?

One of Every Three

According to the National Institutes of Health, between 2007 and 2012, anxiety disorders in children and teens went up 20 percent. Now, nearly one in three of all adolescents will experience an anxiety or mental health disorder.

One in three!

These stats, combined with the fact that the rate of hospital admissions for suicidal teenagers has doubled over the past decade,[14] should have us realizing we all know several people who are suffering from anxiety, depression, or another mental health–related issue.

Years ago, people may have assumed it was only the kids with the blue hair. They would have been wrong then just like they are now. The earbuds, lack of attention, and sullen attitude might be a slightly better indicator of some struggles, but if you think *those* are the prerequisite to mental health struggles, you're still wrong.

---

14 https://www.healthychildren.org/English/health-issues/conditions/emotional-problems/Pages/Anxiety-Disorders.aspx

So who are they? Who are the one in three? They're ...

the boy who's great at making kids laugh at the
lunch table;
the girl who seems like she has it all: perfect grades,
friends, clothes;
the teacher everyone loves;
or the quarterback of the football team.

Long gone are the days when a kid choosing to look
different meant they were suffering from anxiety or
depression.

But, if they aren't just coming out and telling someone they're depressed—and let's face it, most kids (or
adults) aren't—how can we figure it out?

I have a suggestion.

Just Look Up!

There's an African proverb that says, "To go fast, go
alone. To go far, go together."

We were not meant to navigate this world alone; we
were meant to navigate it together. Taking time to

intentionally unplug from our screens allows us to be present and connect deeply with the most important element of *any of our* tribes . . . the people. Goodness thrives when we're in connection with each other, and that connection doesn't exist if we're looking down all day long.

When we look up, we see where our kindness and compassion can be used to make an impact on someone else. Really making a connection with someone—having a conversation about what interests them, smiling at them, listening to their story—is a vital part of helping those around us who are struggling to feel seen and understood. Even if it doesn't heal the pain of what they are going through, it's the only way to know if they need help in the first place.

Just ask Sam.

Think about all the time we spend on trivial stuff that makes no real difference in this world.

I'm not saying it's all a waste, because let's be honest: if you've ever been stuck in line at the DMV for hours, or delayed at an airport, or sitting on a commode, having something trivial to do serves a purpose.

However, in our current landscape, trivial is trumping connection.

Go to a busy restaurant on a Friday night and observe the people at the tables around you. Are they checked in with each other, making eye contact, and having a conversation? Or are they checked out on their phones? In my experience, it's often the latter.

And again, I'm not saying we have to be—or that it's even healthy to be—constantly "on" or in connection, but when leveling up on Candy Crush or checking our social media status fills more of our time than compassion and connection, we need to make some seismic shifts.

The same kind of shifts we made when it came to cigarettes in hospitals and airplanes.

What if, instead of 7.5 entertainment hours a day on our screens, we spent two? Which, for what it's worth, is what social scientists right now say is the amount of time children can spend on screens without increasing the likelihood they'll experience a host of detrimental impacts.[15]

---

15   Twenge, Dr. Jean. *iGen: Why Today's Super-Connected Kids Are Growing Up Less Rebellious, More Tolerant, Less Happy—and Completely Unprepared for Adulthood—and What That Means for the Rest of Us*

And what if you used those extra 5.5 hours every day to actually see the world around you, to actually connect with other human beings in a way that is meaningful?

Not only would it positively change the game for people here and now . . . it would impact our legacy for centuries.

Our Legacy

Societies are often described by the cultural norms that bind people together over a long period of time.

The Stone Age got its name from the prehistoric use of stone tools.
The Renaissance was known for its renewed focus on learning and the arts.
The Age of Enlightenment was an intellectual and philosophical movement filled with innovation.

What will be said about this era? How will we be defined? I believe if we're not careful, we will forever be known as the Age of Disconnection.

Is that what we really want to be remembered for? Not me.

With a little bit of intentionality, courage, and discipline, combined with a whole lot of love, belonging, and hope, I believe this era could be known as something else.

The Age of Human Connection.

Friends, we're going to need a multifaceted approach, because the frightening increase in mental health issues is part of a multifaceted problem.

However, I'm staking my claim on the fact that the most important solution to the problem just happens to be the one all of us can contribute toward.

Human connection . . . *authentic* human connection.

All of us can say "yes" to

a smile at a stranger,
a wave to a neighbor,
or a simple conversation with a grandparent.

It's taking a literal ten seconds out of your day to acknowledge the humans that are sharing the tiny corner of this planet you all call home.

THIS is what authentic human connection looks like!
And all of us can say "yes" to it.

Want to increase happiness?
Reduce our addictions to our screens?
Lower the 33 percent diagnosed with anxiety and
depression?
Leave a stronger legacy?

Just. Look. Up.

Caveman Wisdoms: Just Look Up

Do you like donuts? Me too! They're hard to say no
to. And let's be honest. A donut or two . . . heck, even
three . . . is not going to do all that much damage.

A few donuts, not bad.
Lots of donuts, kind of bad.
Lots of donuts all day, every day . . . really bad.

Phones and computers are no different. It's hard to
say no. They're very tempting, and just like donuts,

a few hours on a screen, not bad.
Many hours on a screen, kind of bad.
Many hours on a screen all day, every day . . .
really bad.

And even though we know the results of overindulging in donuts or screens, or anything for that matter, that doesn't make those things any less tempting.

Therefore, as a family or even as an individual, I think it is imperative that you have a plan for moderation or, if nothing else, boundaries around your screen usage.

It doesn't have to be perfect, and it shouldn't be set in stone. It can, and should, evolve. But it should be something that at least says, "We're conscious about how much time we're looking down."

Happy Caveman has put together a template we call "The Caveman Screen Plan." Print out the template at www.JustLookUpBook.com. I use it in my home with my family. Use it, tweak it, change it, modify it. Here it is:

N^2
S^2
C^2

N^2 = Non-Negotiables

The Happy Caveman Screen Plan has a couple of Non-Negotiables. These are the "no matter what" sort of guidelines.

You only get a few of these, so make sure you choose wisely. I would recommend no more than two or three.

For instance, in my family, the three current N^2s are:

No social media until you're in eighth grade.
No screens in the bedroom after 10:00 p.m.
No more than two hours of gaming.

Maybe the best part of having a few Non-Negotiables is the arguments they prevent! The other day, my seventh-grade daughter begged me to download TikTok. I just shrugged my shoulders like *my hands are tied here* and said "Sorry, our rule is no social media until eighth grade." Although she continued on arguing that she was the only one who doesn't have it, and how she just doesn't understand, I never felt the need to raise my voice, and a long (and possibly ugly) argument was avoided.

S^2 = Sacred Spaces

Sacred Spaces are locations, events, or even days of the week where screens are not allowed. The intention is to preserve places of importance where connection usually happens.

Our S^2 is the dinner table. This is especially important to my wife, so we don't allow anyone to have their phone at a meal, even on silent.

Maybe your sacred space is on a date night, at a sporting event or a happy hour with friends, or even a specific day of the week. (Sundays are awesome!) Either way, giving yourself the permission to have a few sacred areas in your life where technology isn't allowed is a gift you're giving not only to your own brain, but also to the people you are with!

C^2 = *Create Connections*

The first two parts of our plan include ways to allow for human connection by creating time and space for conversation and meaningful interaction.

But listen. Phones aren't going away, and they aren't evil . . . we just want to lessen their impact. Your kid loves their phone. They love their apps, and they love their games. And truth be told, even though they may not tell you this, they want YOU to love what THEY love!

The Caveman Screen Plan includes setting aside time to Create Connections with your kids on the very thing that caused you to create a plan. However, turn this around, and make it an important time by stepping into your kids' world and allowing them to be the teacher, the genius.

Once a week, or whatever works with your schedule, I suggest you do one of the following with your kids:

- Make a TikTok

- Build on Minecraft together

- Watch a YouTube video that makes them laugh

- Draft a Madden team

or anything that allows you to connect with them and allows them to take the lead.

I know these aren't hard-and-fast rules for how to be successful at looking up. The truth is, there are no universal rules that will work for everyone in this regard. But if our shared goal is to spend more time looking up, more time connecting, these guidelines should help create a mindset that allows both to happen more frequently.

CHAPTER FOUR

Fail On

For many years after college, I was a working actor in the Twin Cities, my hometown.

Granted, I had a full-time job—a career, actually, as a youth speaker for a large organization—but after regular work hours and on my days off, I would audition for . . . well, honestly, pretty much anything.

There were commercials, films, voiceovers, industrials (those in-house training videos companies like Best Buy and Target show employees when they get hired), product plugs, and about a hundred other opportunities. Some paid well. Some did not.

ALL were incredibly time consuming.

You see, it was not just one audition. It was . . .

1 audition
+ 1 callback
+ <u>1-3 days of waiting in agony as they made a decision</u>
Getting a role approximately 1 percent of the time.

Then, if you *were* the one chosen, it was

   1 day of wardrobe/fittings
+ 1 day (at least) of memorizing the script
+ <u>1 day of shooting</u>
A whole lot of days for a side hustle that may or may not have been paying you well, but that you loved and hoped would eventually land you a bigger role, so you kept doing it.

You can probably imagine my delight when I received the call from my agent that I had been chosen for a gig **without needing to go to any audition.**

I was going to make ALL the money for a fraction of the normal work!

"So, you're telling me that after taking one glance at my headshot [the incredibly large/awkward close-up of an actor's face], they knew I was their guy?" I asked.

"I know, right?!" said my agent, in shared disbelief.

I couldn't believe my luck!

"Wow! That's amazing. What's it for?" I asked.

"Well . . ." She paused before continuing, "It's not your typical on-camera commercial."

It was technically a modeling gig. But instead of my face being in a magazine, I was going to be on a giant billboard on the side of the highway, advertising the grand reopening of a mall.

"Thousands of people are going to drive by your face every single day," she told me excitedly before she hung up the phone.

Wow!
With *one* look,
At *one* picture
Of *my one* face,

They knew I was their . . . say it with me . . . **model**!

I was going to be like Brad Pitt or Taye Diggs, or actor

and face of lifeguards everywhere David Hasselhoff (don't Hassel the Hoff)!

Incredible! All this hard work was starting to pay off.

On the day of the shoot, I showed up early to the set. Punctuality and ridiculously good modeling didn't need to be mutually exclusive talents.

When I stepped out of my car, Amanda, the person in charge of hiring the talent, spotted me right away.

Obviously, she knew who I was.

"Hi, Joe!" she said, greeting me with a big smile.

Then, she pulled out a walkie-talkie to communicate with her team. "OK, guys, we're going to start in about thirty minutes!"

She then looked at me, smiled, and said excitedly to her walkie-talkie, "And good news, the Nerd is here."

She handed me a pocket protector and said, "Keep this for the shoot."

As she walked away, she looked back and said, "I knew we got the right guy."

Whoa, whoa, whoa! You mean to tell me that

with *one* look,
at *one* picture
of *my one* face,

I was handed the role of . . . THE NERD?!?

For three entire months, thousands of people drove by that billboard every day and saw my face, accompanied by my slicked-down hair (parted in the middle), a shirt buttoned to the very top button (with a pocket protector), and black-rimmed glasses (with masking tape in the middle). The Nerd, inviting them to come see the new mall.

Awesome.

Plethora of Failures

I'm not going to lie. The hardest part about writing a chapter on failure was trying to figure out which story I should tell. I have several (thousand) to choose from.

There was the time where I:

- had my fly wide open in front of hundreds of people in a stage production

- embarrassed myself in front of Liz Walker by farting while doing sit-ups in gym class

- forgot nearly every word of my entire talk on my first international speaking gig

- embarrassed myself in front of Emily Yanez when she caught me daydreaming about her in class

- took my parents' car out when I was fifteen and got pulled over by the cops

- embarrassed myself in front of Gianna, the beautiful concession stand worker at the Metrodome, when I was in ninth grade

There's a pattern here with women, if you didn't notice.

You see, unlike some topics where content is scarce, failure provides me with an abundance of options.

My guess is if you're willing to be honest with yourself, it does for you too.

My other guess is if you had to choose between telling someone a story about a giant failure in your life and sticking a hot poker in your eye, you'd have to take some time and think hard about it.

The reason? We have the wrong mindset.

No Fail

The title of this chapter (and Phrase #4) is Fail On, but so many of us get fed a different phrase from very early on. Instead of Fail On, it's No Fail.

For so many, the messages that slowly get pounded into our heads, or that we begin at some point to tell ourselves, are:

Failure is negative;
vulnerability is a weakness;
any mishap, stumble, mistake, or screw-up
should be avoided at all costs.

No Fail! No Fail! No Fail!

Need proof? Go take a look at someone's Instagram feed. There's a very small chance you're going to see anything but perfect poses with laughing friends and filters that cover up every flaw.

The problem with avoiding failures at all costs and covering up all the flaws is that what's left isn't real. And if we want to keep up with it all, we have to continue the exhausting facade.

Like a hammer slowly tapping on a large glass, the No Fail mindset starts chipping away at our confidence. We start judging ourselves, and as I wrote about in chapter 1, the comparison game begins . . . and we've already been through how futile comparison is.

And so . . .

Rather than pursuing our passions,
    we stick to what's safe.

Rather than trying out for the team,
    we choose to stay home.

Rather than raise our hand in class,
  we sit quietly in the corner.

I see a lot of potential wasted in the pursuit of perfection. And the consequence of this pursuit is a lifetime of regret. We don't get time back.

The spoken-word artist Prince Ea summarized the results of a study of one hundred elderly people who, at the end of their life, were asked about their biggest regret. An excerpt from his poem "Everybody Dies but Not Everybody Lives" says,

Facing death, close to their last breath
They were asked to reflect on life's biggest regret

Nearly all of them said,
they regretted not the things they did,
but the things they didn't do.
The risks they never took,
the dreams they didn't pursue.

I ask you, will your last words be "If only I had . . ."?

I meet a lot of students who live in constant fear

because they know they're only a few more taps away from being completely shattered.

Students like Logan.

Everyone's Broken

One time, I was sharing some stories about some of my not-so-positive high school experiences and habits. I had given this talk on numerous occasions, but this time was different. Afterward, a young man named Logan walked up to me and shared some things that were pretty dark.

I listened, as I do to all stories from students like this, intently.

However, he said something at the end of the conversation that was different than what I'm used to hearing.

"I think what I've realized by hearing your stories is *everyone's* broken."

And it's not so much what he said, but rather how he said it. He said "everyone's broken" with a hint of acceptance, of understanding. It was like a light bulb in his head got switched on for the very first time, and instead of being hopeless, Logan was actually hopeful.

And he went on to say . . .

"For so long I've always thought it was just me, but I'm realizing it's everyone, even a guy like you."

In that moment, Logan's mindset went from *No Fail!* to *Fail On!* With that one short sentence—"I'm realizing it's everyone"—I could tell that Logan got it!

Everyone's broken. Everyone fails.

We think we're the only ones, but we're not.

Whether you're the quarterback or the valedictorian or the kid that doesn't seem to have even a single friend (let alone a real group to hang out with), know this: we all have our failures. Our mishaps. Our stumbles. Our screw-ups. We all have failed in a way that deeply embarrasses us to this day.

And maybe the only difference between those who

"make it" and those who don't is their ability to own those failures.

Medal of Scars

The great author Paulo Coelho says, "I don't regret my painful times, I bare my scars as if they were medals."

I love this mentality because it tells us to embrace our failures. Own our embarrassments.

Bare them.
Expose them. Make them visible.
Like medals.

That's powerful.

Fail On is the mentality of those who embrace their failures. Who own their struggles. Who take their mistake, mishap, or screw-up, and use it as fuel to make themselves better, stronger, and wiser.

What happens when people employ the Fail On mindset in their lives? Let's see . . .

During their winning season, the US women's soccer team, arguably the best soccer team in our country's history, had a picture of their last great defeat posted near the exit of their locker room, so it was the last thing they saw walking out to the pitch every night.

Fail On!

Walt Disney was fired from the *Kansas City Star* because his editor felt he "lacked imagination and had no good ideas."

Fail On!

Oprah Winfrey was abruptly fired from one of her early jobs on TV after the producer declared she was "unfit for television."

Fail On!

Author J. K. Rowling had twelve major publishers reject the manuscript for *Harry Potter and the Philosopher's Stone*.

Fail On!

Michael Jordan missed seventy-two game-winning shot opportunities in his career as the greatest player in NBA history. He also got cut from his varsity basketball team.

Fail On!

Beyoncé Knowles was told that she didn't have what it took to be in entertainment.

Fail On!

Albert Einstein was told by his teachers that he would never amount to anything.

Fail On!

Are you catching the pattern here?

Besides the obvious Fail On mindset, there's something else. Every single one of them had haters. Doubters. People who didn't believe they could accomplish the things they were passionate about accomplishing. And not a single one of these people allowed those haters to have the last word.

The truth is, you're going to have haters too. My guess is that you've already met one or two, or a hundred; there will always be people in your life who cut you down. Unfortunately, it's sometimes the people you care about the most,

a sibling,
a best friend,
a coach,

who belittle your worth or don't see the potential you possess.

As painful as that can be, the million-dollar question is, will you believe them? The No Fail mindset certainly hopes you do—because just like the NEs in chapter 1, it will find any excuse to keep you small. However, the Fail On mindset acknowledges that haters exist but never allows them to get the last word.

Minion Love

For three straight months, my large, nerdy face was plastered on one of the busiest stretches of highway in the Twin Cities.

Awesome.

But instead of avoiding it, I decided to embrace it. To bear it like a medal.

The next time I got called to go to an audition, I failed. And the next time. And the time after that, and honestly, the next fifty-four times after that. Fifty-seven failures in a row! That's a whole lot of failing!

But then came audition number fifty-eight.

My agent, the one who'd booked me for the nerd billboard, called me and said, "Best Buy is interested in having you read for a spot they're going to put in the trailers for this new movie called *Despicable M*e." She went on to say there were these things called "Minions" in the movie, and they would be part of the commercial.

"What are my chances?"

She point-blank responded, "Probably not that good."

But since it would be a national spot, and the audition was local, I decided it might be worth the effort. I went.

Three weeks later, as I got off a plane to speak in Montana for my full-time job, my agent called to tell me that I got the part.[16]

This was huge!

Even though it was years after earning my degree, it felt like my choice of a theater major was finally validated. I was proud of this, and my family was too. It felt like a win for all the hard work I'd put into pursuing acting for years. Not to mention, it was an incredibly cool experience I'll never forget.

Little Victories

ALL of us have failed and will continue to fail in the future. The question isn't "Will I fail?" but "Will I choose to avoid it, or will I embrace it?" If you do embrace it (and I hope you do), what wisdom will

---

16   If you're interested in seeing me and a couple of Minions advertise a Best Buy app, you can find the thirty-second ad at www.JustLookUpBook. com.

you gain so you don't repeat the same failure over and over?

Ultimately, that's the hope.

Just like a baby learning to walk, the hope is that eventually, with each failure, we will learn how to improve.

The hope shouldn't be to strive for or try to maintain this false notion of perfection. It's simply to make micro-improvements every day, as a result of every experience, so you can be a little bit better tomorrow than you were today. Little victories.

And the only way to make that happen is to stumble, fall, mess up, screw up. And then embrace it, learn from it, grow, and move on.

The only way to make that happen is to choose to Fail On!

Side note: here's the rest of the story about that Best Buy commercial.

As I mentioned, my steady, full-time job was as a

youth speaker. I'd been doing that the whole time I was also auditioning and acting. The truth is, I loved both jobs, and over the years, I felt like I'd gotten pretty good at being a motivational speaker.

I knew I couldn't do both of them forever, and even though the Best Buy commercial was my biggest role yet, I had a choice to make.

It was clear acting wasn't going to fit my young family's lifestyle. Plus, I loved working with young people.

So I decided to go out on a high note—I made that commercial the last thing I did as a professional actor. I don't at all feel like I failed at acting just because I didn't end up making it my career. I got to do something I loved for years, and it taught me valuable lessons about how to Fail On in the best possible ways.

When you commit to living by Fail On as a mindset, you're bound to eventually succeed.

And when you do, the prize is likely going to feel that much sweeter!

Phrase #4 . . . FAIL ON!

Caveman Wisdoms: Fail On

Maybe the single greatest tool we have in our "human connection toolbox" is storytelling. Did you know that the normal teenager is in daydream mode nearly 50 percent of the day?[17] It's true!

Our minds are constantly bombarded with a plethora of information, which means that subconsciously, our brain is working overtime to keep up with all the filing/organizing/sorting, etc. . . .

While this subconscious organization is happening behind the scenes, on the main stage, we're dreaming about life on a beach, or what's going to be for dinner that night, or "Do I have a booger . . . OMG I think I have a booger!"

We're thinking about all those things and so much more, except during a story.

There's something about a phrase like "Once upon a time . . ." or "That reminds me of that one time when . . ." that captures the human brain. Struggling to

---

17   https://www.nola.com/entertainment_life/health_fitness/
article_659cb6d2-2567-504d-915f-23ae78237a59.html

make a connection with your students, kids, friends? Use the power of story to help break through!

If you would have asked me eighteen years ago what stories would have the biggest impact on an audience, I would have said the ones

where I knocked it out of the park,
or when I did the right thing,
or when everyone else did the wrong thing and I did the right thing.

I would have sworn those would be the stories people related to best, the ones they wanted to hear.

Those stories are good. And they have their place in making connections with others. But the stories that really move the needle, the ones the audience always nods in agreement with, are the ones where I have fallen on my face. When I said the wrong thing, or did something that made me shudder in embarrassment. These are the stories that make us real, the stories that make us human.

We ALL have these stories of our humanness: the

good, the bad, and the ugly. And the truth is, those around us want to hear them.

It may feel strange at first, or you may feel like you don't have any stories to share. I have an acronym I like to use when I'm leading storytelling sessions that will prompt some ideas. I recommend that families use this around the dinner table, or teachers use it for class meetings or writing prompts.

The acronym is called FORDS.

FORDS stands for
Family
Occupation
Recreation
Dreams
School

Let's use the family dinner table as our example. Introduce these five areas in our lives that generally produce a lot of our stories. Have people think of an example from one of these areas and be ready to tell their story . . . it can be brief or detailed, whatever you want. Then, take turns sharing.

The goal is simply to connect, as humans, around our stories. To discover new things about people we know and love, and to bond around the things we have in common with or can relate to in one another.

Here's a bit more detail about these five areas:

Family: They say you can't pick your family. However, what you can do is share stories about them! Think back to childhood—to a time when new siblings or cousins were born, or to the family vacation that started out with a flat tire that Dad changed on the side of the road. What were family dinners like when you were a kid? Remember that time Aunt Beth caught the dish towel on fire?

Occupation: We've all had first days, last days, good days, stressful days. Days where we wanted to quit, and days when it all felt right. Part-time jobs to careers, our work and our coworkers fill our days with stories to tell.

Recreation: What do/did you love doing outside of work or school? My physics teacher in high school, Mr. Westlake, started every one of his classes with a story, and many of those were about his motorcycle.

He LOVED riding his motorcycle, and we loved hearing about it. What you do for recreation is a direct reflection of what you're passionate about, and passion is extremely contagious!

Dreams: We've all dreamt of places we want to go, people we want to meet, accomplishments we want to achieve. What are yours now? What were they when you were younger? Did you accomplish them? Did you try something and then have to change course?

School: If *any* of these five options will instantly and forever resonate with youth, it's stories about the location where they spend nearly half their waking hours for nine months out of the year . . . school. You could probably write a whole book on your stories from your time in the halls/bus/classroom/locker room/field/court/stage and everywhere in between. Again, be real about the good, the bad, and the outright embarrassing.

My guess is there are a lot of fantastic successes, as well as a lot of Fail On moments, within all five of these categories for every person reading this book.

The goal isn't for you to write a book (unless that's

your thing . . . then write away!). The goal is simply to tell your story, however you'd like. Have conversations if you prefer, or write something in a letter to a loved one if that's your style.

Whatever option you choose, share your stories, so more of us can Fail On together!

CHAPTER FIVE

Yeah Toast!

OK . . .

So we've made it this far together. The bond between us is growing stronger. Do you feel it? I certainly do.

Phrase #1: Love YOU
Phrase #2: Push Through
Phrase #3: Just Look Up
Phrase #4: Fail On

Which brings us to the fifth and final phrase in this book: Yeah Toast!

Yeah Toast? What in the world?

Let me tell you a little story. It's a favorite of mine.

On a typical day, if you peeked into my life and home, you'd see

laundry piled high,
pee on the bathroom floors (seriously . . . boys . . .),
and the kids running around the neighborhood
(pants optional for my youngest).

Just a little truth in parenting for ya.

Most days, it's a hot mess, and my wife Jess and I
work all day long to keep it all functioning. Would I
trade it? No. Is it perfect? Also no.

I love ALL my children (most days), and although I
don't have the space in this book to write a chapter
highlighting each one's unique brilliance, I feel com-
pelled to take a minute to tell you about my middle
guy, Finn.

Finn has this amazing, joy-filled spirit.

He dances.

He dabs, which I'm sure he'll deeply regret later, but
for now, dab on, my man!

When Finn was three, he loved making breakfast.
Specifically toast.

He would run downstairs on his chunky little legs, put the bread in the toaster, and wait and wait and wait,

and watch and watch and watch.

And the bread would, you know,

toast and toast and toast.

When it popped up, Finn would look at me, eyes wide, with this amazing look of surprise on his face like, *Whoa . . . I had NO idea that was coming!*

Then, he would raise his hands in the air and shriek as if he had just won the lottery.

And I was always like, "Dude, it's just toast."

And he would look at me almost disappointedly. I could practically hear his little three-year-old self thinking, *No, you idiot . . . it's a miracle!*

Clouds, Puddles, and Toasters

"I love hanging out with three-year-olds. I love hanging out with them because they're seeing the world for the very first time."

–Neil Pasricha

As silly as it sounds, at one point, ALL of us used to cheer for little things that brought us so much joy.

Whether it was finding shapes in the clouds
or broad-jumping into puddles
or cheering for toast,

at some point for all of us,

average was amazing,
mundane was magnificent,
and "No big deal" was "No freaking way!"

And if you let yourself really think about it—like, pull it apart and break it down—most of that stuff actually *is* amazing!

Let's start with clouds . . .

- Did you know the average cloud weighs more than a million pounds in fair weather, and can pack billions—maybe even trillions!—of pounds of water during a thunderstorm?[18]

Think puddle jumping is just random?

- No way! It's been linked to boosting our immune systems and has even received its own official national day (January 16) on the calendar![19]

And toasters . . . don't even get me started . . .

- Did you know that toasters are designed specifically to cook our bread at 310°F, so the sugars from the bread begin to brown and create the crunchy surface?[20] Somebody had to figure that out!

Finn's right! When you think about it, all of it—clouds, puddles, toasters, and so much more—is really, really amazing! That amazingness surrounds us every day. In every area of our lives.

And yet . . . we miss it.

---

18   https://www.mentalfloss.com/article/75190/15-billowing-facts-about-clouds

19   https://hikeitbaby.com/blog/how-jumping-puddles-boost-immune-sytsem/

20   https://quickservant.com/weird-facts-about-toasters/

Every day, hundreds of clouds float boringly over our heads, thousands of puddles lie as still as glass, and seventy-five million people make toast, and not one of them gets the least bit excited about it.

Why are three-year-olds so great at seeing these moments, and why are we so poor at it?

I believe it comes down to two reasons.

Reason #1: Caveman Brains

> *"What the brain does a lot of, the brain gets good at."*
> —Erin Walsh, neuroscientist

Let's take a trip back in time. The year was 25,000 BC. You were a caveperson.

Your job? Not all that different from today. Stay alive.

It was a stressful job, what with all the saber-toothed tigers, sandstorms, and about a thousand other things trying to keep you from making it through another day.

But you didn't succumb to these dangers . . . you survived!

How?

It's because your body had built-in protections that helped keep you safe. We used to think that could all be attributed to one superhero inside your brain called the amygdala. We know now that the amygdala plays a role in fear response, but really, it was a complex system of several networks that helped cave-people know how to react to threats. You still have that same system today.

You see, back in the day, those networks were on the clock 24/7, constantly scanning our environment for anything that could pose a threat, informing us when it made sense to fight the tiger and when it made sense to run.

And with the help of Amygdala and Co., not only did we survive, we thrived!

Twenty-seven thousand years later, we've come a long way. However, those complex fear-detector networks haven't come so far. They're still on high alert 24/7.

All day, every day, they're scanning our environment for anything that could cause us harm. And although we don't have saber-toothed tigers to worry about anymore, we have a new set of threats.

For teachers, it may be:

student well-being,
assessments,
or top-down decision-making.

For parents, the saber-toothed tigers might be:

bedtime routines,
screen time meltdowns,
or other judgy parents.

For students, it's:

What will he think?
What will she think?
What does everyone think?

And just like the NEs we talked about in the first chapter, these threats play over and over in our minds.

No wonder we miss little moments that bring us joy; we're literally wired to be scanning for the negative.

But that's only the first reason.

Reason #2: Hard Knocks

The other reason we miss celebrating the small things harkens back to chapter 2, which reminded us, quite simply, that life is hard. For some, it's really, really hard.

For me, it started with a T-shirt making fun of my appearance,
and then an injury that took away my dream of playing sports,
a false belief that my worth was based on my weight,
and the major embarrassment of being the nerd on a billboard.

These are just a few examples I've mentioned in this book.

There's also that

my grandparents died within six months of each

other, my parents divorced my junior year of high school, and my wife lost her best friend in a car accident.

And of course, even with this whole list, I'm just scratching the surface.

So when you couple together

> ***brains hardwired to be negative +***
> ***lives full of hard knocks,***

you can see how our brains have lots and lots of threats to focus on. Lots of negative. Things like clouds, puddles, and toast aren't even close to being on our radar.

And slowly, over time,

the voice of that little kid,
the one with that spirit, that joy,
the one who used to cheer for little things like the magic of toast,

gets stuffed down, shut down, and replaced by a completely different voice.

Allie the Insecure

A couple of years after starting Happy Caveman, I was speaking at a middle school in central Iowa. I gave my talk in the morning, and if I'm being honest, it was one of my best . . . a much stronger presentation than Blue Hair Girl experienced years prior.

Kids really seemed to connect with the message . . . I had a lot of requests for selfies that day. I was feeling pretty good.

As I often do when I speak in schools for the day, I went to the cafeteria during lunch. I met an eighth-grade girl we'll call Allie when I sat down at her lunch table. She had been in the crowd when I spoke in the morning.

Three things were obvious to me about Allie in about my first fifteen seconds at the table.

1. Allie was cool.
2. Allie had power.
3. Allie was deeply insecure.

With positive curiosity, I asked, "What's for lunch?"

She, with negative disdain, answered, ". . ."

Literally. She just glared at me as her answer.

And although I'm not fluent in the language known as "teenager" anymore, I'm quite certain her response meant either

Shut your face
or
I hate your face
or
I want to punch you in the face.

Hard to know exactly.

In any case, it was pretty obvious she wasn't all that pumped I had chosen to sit at her table, and downright annoyed I had the gumption to attempt to interact with her in any form.

I sat, observing Allie engage with the kids at her table, watching how she talked to her friends. I made a few comments here and there, and Allie's friends responded to me by saying whatever Allie wanted to hear to avoid her making fun of them.

And yet the whole time she was running this show, it was obvious that behind Allie's mask of attitude and apathy, there lived a little kid. One who had hopes and dreams and joy and light. A little girl who used to see what was possible for her life.

Unfortunately, it seemed that voice had been shut down a long time ago, replaced by one that was critical and condescending.

Along with Allie's skeptical Amygdala & Co. response, somewhere, somehow, she had experienced some hard knocks. Rejection, embarrassment, shame, or failure . . . maybe a combination of them all.

Maybe no one had taught her to Fail On, and she felt alone in her mistakes. Or maybe she had heard a chorus of NEs for years, and the way she drowned them out was treating others badly.

Who knows. But now, it was obvious she spent her whole day pretending to be someone she was not.

How many of us have shut down the voice of that little boy or girl that lives inside?

At what age?

For what reason did it become not cool anymore to

dream big
be smart
sit with *that* kid
or even smile?

When did we forget the joy of

making shapes out of clouds
jumping in puddles
toast?

How many of us have turned off our heart or shut down our dreams, all in the name of blending in?

Listen, I'm a realist. At some point, it's time to grow up, move forward, and put the stuffed animals away. It's inevitable.

But I also know, no matter how old we are, our happiness and how we feel about our life are directly tied to where we put our focus.

And when we trade putting our focus on

the good,
the amazing,
the wonder,
and the awe

in exchange for

negative news cycles,
judgments of others,
or popularity and acceptance,

we lose this vital part of our soul, this vital part of our joy and happiness.

And, as a lot of adults will tell you, it can be really hard to get back.

We All Just Want to Be Happy

On that day in central Iowa, I spent the afternoon at the school doing a leadership session with a small group of students. As I was packing up my stuff for the day, preparing to leave, I felt a tap on my shoulder.

Allie.

She blurted out, "I don't want to be remembered as the girl you saw in the lunchroom. That's not who I am," and then, through tears, she whispered, "I just want to be happy."

It was as if the hard, fake shell I saw at lunch had fallen away, and the quivering, innocent voice of that little girl deep inside was back.

I told her the same thing I'll tell all of you: if you want to be truly happy, keep that little kid inside you alive.

Yes . . .

grow up,
move forward,
take risks,
accept new challenges.

And at the same time . . .

Don't forget
to play, and dance, and dab.

Don't forget
to jump in puddles,
make shapes out of clouds,
and laugh uncontrollably with your friends.

Don't forget every once in a while, in the busyness of our world, to slow down, raise your hands in the air, and cheer for the little things that used to bring so much joy to your heart.

And next time your bread magically pops out of the toaster, magically transformed into toast at a perfect 310°F, with those sugars crystallized to form the crunch you love, I want you to be like Finn and raise your hands in the air and shriek, "YEAH TOAST!"

P.S. Some of you might be wondering about Allie, or Sam, or any of the other students I mention in this book. I wonder about them too.

I meet a lot of students like Allie. Students whose "light bulb of life" turns on the day that I speak at their school. One of the hardest parts of this job is that oftentimes, I don't get to see what happens next. However, I have to believe that this Yeah Toast! message—or any of the others—is something that students like Allie will remember, and continue to apply in different areas of their life, for a very long time.

My heart tells me, based on my eighteen years of experience and the tone of her voice in our final conversation, that Allie is going to be all right!

Caveman Wisdoms: Yeah Toast!

For Phrase #5, I have something for you to work on that will help you train your brain to see the small things worth celebrating, and in turn, help you stay focused on the positive.

It's a practice called the Attitude of Gratitude.

Practice?

Yes, practice. Like any other thing we want to be better at doing, we have to practice seeing the small things and being grateful for them.

So how do we do this? There are two parts. Both are short, intentional activities that prime our brains and hearts to look for the good.

Step One: Start a daily gratitude journal.

It doesn't need to be fancy; just a small, simple note-book will do. Put it next to your bed with a pen.

At the end of every day, think through what you did, what you saw, or who you spoke to.

Make a list of three things you're grateful for.

1.
2.
3.

That's it!

This isn't about creating long, beautiful paragraphs about every day. It's just meant to give you practice in seeing the little things that bring joy.

Because while every day might not be magnificent and packed with amazing events, there are little things to celebrate, like shapes in clouds, a quick splash in a puddle, or crunchy toast.

Step Two: Write a letter.

When I speak to students, I often say, "It's not about changing the world, it's about changing one person's day."

What better way to change a person's day than to write them a letter?

Again, this doesn't need to take you days to write. Simply think of someone who you should thank, or who has done something worth congratulating, and write them a letter.

Not only will you make their day, you'll reap benefits too.

A leading researcher in the field of positive psychology, Dr. Martin Seligman, tested the impact of various positive psychology interventions on over 400 people.[21] The single most influential intervention was the one he dubbed "The Letter Challenge."

Half the group was challenged to write and personally deliver a letter of gratitude to someone who had never been properly thanked for his or her kindness. Those who wrote the letter immediately exhibited a

---

21   https://www.brainpickings.org/2014/02/18/martin-seligman-gratitude-visit-three-blessings/

huge increase in happiness scores, with benefits lasting for a month.

Incredible, right? Retraining your brain to see the positives ends up benefiting those around you in addition to yourself. It's a win-win!

CHAPTER SIX

The One in Three

As we wrap up (parting is such sweet sorrow), I want to share how I use the Five Phrases in my own life, specifically with my seventh-grade daughter, Sophia.

Four years ago, when Sophia was in third grade, I received a message from her school nurse, Mrs. Prescher. It read something along the lines of:

> *Dear Mr. Beckman,*
> *I don't quite know how to say this, but your daughter Sophia is coming into my office on a daily basis. Based on what she's been sharing, I have some significant concerns that she is struggling with something bigger than you may know. I suggest you have her evaluated for a handful of mental health–related concerns I see.*

Obviously, this was a difficult email to receive.

I remember my initial reaction being, *"She's got the*

wrong person! I mean, doesn't she know that the very girl she is talking about is the daughter of a motivational speaker, who talks about a lot of this stuff in hundreds of schools every year?"

But then, it all started to make sense. As I reflected on Sophia's behavior patterns over the few months before the email, it hit me: Mrs. Prescher knew exactly what she was talking about.

Shortly after that email, we took Sophia to see a specialist, and she was diagnosed with childhood depression.

My Sophia was the one in three.

Even after she was diagnosed and started to get the help she needed, there were a lot of tears and long nights. In fourth grade, she missed nearly thirty days of school. Some days, she couldn't get out of bed.

Over the last four years, she's become very well equipped to understand her symptoms and ask for help when she needs it. Her mom and I are also much more aware of how and when to help.

I don't share Sophia's story to make you feel bad for her or me, or to tug at your heartstrings. I decided, with Sophia's permission, to share her story in this book and from the stage because she is, in so many ways, the poster child for mental health today.

On the outside, she looks like everything is fine. Her home life is stable. She lives in a safe neighborhood. She attends a good school, and she has friends. She doesn't get in trouble. No one would suspect she deals with this, unless they knew her really well and knew she'd missed so much school in fourth grade.

I share Sophia's story to open your eyes to the reality of what this looks like today.

The Five Phrases Applied

Phrase #1, Love YOU, is the basis for the self-worth I'm trying to help Sophia see she has. Teenage years can be really difficult in this area, and even more challenging when you're also dealing with mental health struggles. We use this language a lot. This child is in touch with her NEs!

Phrase #2, Push Through, helps us on the harder

days. We don't ignore what's causing her pain or anxiety, but we do try to equip her with the skills she needs to be resilient.

Phrase #3, Just Look Up, is for both of us. For Sophia, that means making sure her screen time is appropriately limited. For me, it's a reminder that there is zero chance for me to connect with her or notice a problem if I'm buried in a screen. When Sophia is hurting the worst, she doesn't need someone to try to magically make her problems go away. She just needs us to see her, talk to her, and try to understand her.

Phrase #4, Fail On, is a reminder that everyone fails, not just someone diagnosed with depression, and not just kids. Failure is often where the learning happens. I share my own mistakes with her, and I help her see her way through her own missteps.

Phrase #5, Yeah Toast!, helps us remember to celebrate the small joys in life and express gratitude for them. And we practice every night at dinner. After a short prayer, everyone shares one thing they are grateful for. Sound corny? It's not. It forces Sophia to see the little joys in life. I believe when we see good, we feel good, and when we feel good, we do good.

Four years ago, when my work life and home life collided like this, I wasn't immediately sure what to do beyond getting Sophia the medical help she needed. Then I remembered the messages from students, and their teachers, telling me story after story about how these phrases had worked in their lives. And I knew then that I needed to put these phrases into practice even more than I previously had.

As I mentioned at the start, I don't claim that the Five Phrases will be the elixir that will cure all of your or your family's pain. For some of you, all five will resonate; for others, it may be just a couple, or maybe even a small piece within one of the phrases.

Whatever the case, if any of the phrases or parts of them resonate with you, your kids, or anyone else in your life, I urge you to find a way to use them, apply them, and breathe life into them.

I know that in ten years the Five Phrases might very well shift into a whole different Five Phrases because …

life is always changing, shifting, evolving;
hard knocks will continue to present themselves in

different forms;
and pain will surround us everywhere we go.

One thing that will never change, though,
is the fact that
the hardships
the celebrations
life

are better when we're in connection with each other.

Communities, tribes, neighborhoods, and friends all provide the one thing our lives need at a cellular level: human connection. So if nothing else, use this book to somehow, in some way, increase the connection you have with your tribe.

Because ultimately, the most important phrase of all is this last one ... HUMAN CONNECTION MATTERS.

Epilogue

Before we end, I have one final story.

About five years ago, I was sitting in my kitchen around 10:00 p.m. I was enjoying one thing that dads with three young children rarely get . . .

peace and quiet.

All of a sudden, the silence was broken by a ding from my phone.

It was a message from a student, and it read like this:

> *Hi–you were at my school about a week ago, and I tried to DM you, but it didn't work. So . . . hi. I feel bad I couldn't do this in person, but I just wanted to say "thank you so much." I tried an act of courage. I sat in the cafeteria for the first time in forever. Which may not seem like a lot, but it is to me. Today I ignored all the people trying to drag me down, and I ate, and kept it all down. And it all actually went OK.*

So . . . thank you so much for existing :)

Whoa. Tears. I'm the kind of guy who cries at touching commercials. You can only imagine the puddles of tears after receiving this.

After I regained my composure, I thought, "Who would have taken the time to write me this? What student did I have such a strong connection with that they would have opened up about something so personal?"

So I clicked on the profile page.

And lo and behold . . .

It was Blue Hair Girl.

Whoa.

Let's be clear. Blue Hair Girl didn't reach out because I gave an awesome talk. Like I mentioned, it was a "C" at best.

I'm certain she took the time to connect with me because I took the time to make a connection with her.

As promised in the introduction, Blue Hair Girl's life was not radically changed after hearing me talk. But she took in the message, realized I was genuine when I stopped to chat with her, and then had the courage to take one small step for herself.

I always say, "It's not about changing the world, it's about changing one person's day."

No one act of human connection on its own is going to change the world, but if all of us made

one connection
with one person
every day,
and we added those together . . .

that's how we'd change the world.

And that's the challenge. For all of us to do our part. Use our gifts. Invest in our passions. Somehow, in some way, make our world better tomorrow than it was today.

I believe without a doubt that begins with Human Connection! *Grunt!*

Acknowledgments

I would be a fool not to start this section without thanking my abnormally awesome family.

My wife Jess is a complete and total rock star who wears the pants, runs the show, and somehow keeps my head above water. I'm certain her life consists of twenty-five-hour days versus the mere twenty-four the rest of us get. There's just no way she could possibly do as much as she does, and stay as patient along the way, if this were not the case. She is my/our #CaveMama, and without her commitment, NONE of this is possible. I love you, JJ.

I also have three little Cavekiddos as well: Sophia (13), Finn (9), and Jonah (7). As I mentioned in chapter 5, each of them has their own unique brilliance, but all share the beautiful hearts and kind souls of their great-grandmother, to whom this book is dedicated. I love you, kiddos, more than you'll ever know. I'm so proud to be able to call myself your dad.

Next is Scott Kollmann. As mentioned in the

introduction, Scott is my business partner and the cofounder of Happy Caveman. The only reason I had the time to write this book is because Scott was taking care of the marketing, sales, accounting, web design, apparel, and everything else that is happening with the business . . . including the new role of "keep us afloat even during a pandemic."

Next is Nicole Pals-Diehl. I met Nicole five years ago at a conference in Atlanta, Georgia. There were at least seven different occasions where we got on or off the elevator at the exact same time. Finally, I went, "Hmmm . . . maybe the universe is trying to connect us." Good call!

One of Nicole's strengths and passions, it turns out, is editing. She's also uber talented at writing. Both of those skills are prevalent in the pages of this book. Nicole took what was a decent manuscript and helped mold it into a really good book. Yes, these are my stories, from my perspective, and my talking points. However, I learned pretty early on that I could only do so much with all that stuff. I needed someone to breathe a different set of energy into both the stories and the lessons that accompany them. Nicole was that life! If anything resonates with you in this book, there's a 100 percent chance Nicole had something to do with making that happen.

Teachers (from ALL walks of life)

I wouldn't be able to sleep at night if I didn't at some point in this book take some time to honor the beautiful humans who own the esteemed role of "teacher."

Whether you're a classroom teacher, counselor, paraprofessional, administrator, nurse, custodian, bus driver, or anyone in between, you're a teacher. I believe ANYONE who works in education and has the ability to impact a kid is a teacher.

Listen, and please listen closely . . . you have the most important job on this planet, and in the mind of *this* Caveman, it's not even close.

Businessman Lee Iacocca says, "In a completely rational society, the best of us would be teachers, and the rest of us would have to settle for something less, because passing civilization along from one generation to the next ought to be the highest honor and the highest responsibility anyone could have."

I couldn't agree more.

The truth is, my daughter's improvement had less to do with

a doctor
or a drug
or a dad

and a whole lot more to do with Nurse Prescher in third grade and her teacher Mrs. Patty in fifth.

Their ability (one of many) to show genuine compassion and kindness, as well as provide a little bit of tough love, was the exact equation Sophia and our family needed. They made school feel like a safe place for her, and Sophia wanted to be there. Our entire family will forever be grateful for that.

If you're a teacher and you're reading these words right now, please hear me when I say, with the deepest sincerity, thank you.

Whether you know it or not, you are very likely the Mrs. Patty or Nurse Prescher for at least one kiddo in your life. Probably many more.

To the students . . .

We're living in uncertain times. And the truth is, it might feel uncertain for many years to come.

Every generation will deal with its own challenges. You're no different.

And although I don't know what specifically brought you to this book, my guess is that it's the desire to somehow make whatever challenges you face a little easier.

I believe employing at least one of the Five Phrases:

Love YOU
Push Through
Just Look Up
Fail On
Yeah Toast!

will serve you on your quest.

And you want to know what excites me the most?

You.

I'm excited about you guys. I'm excited about your energy, your passion, and your willingness to make a difference. I'm excited to see what you will do in this world.

No doubt you will, at times, question whether your work to change the world is worth it.

Am I really making an impact?
Am I truly leaving a legacy?

I assure you, you are, if you are trying to make the world just a little bit better for yourselves and others.

Joe

Book Joe to Speak!

Over the last nineteen years, Joe Beckman has spoken in educational settings all over the world with one simple mission: to reclaim human connection.

If you're looking for a . . .

- Conference keynote
- Professional development training
- Student session
- Parent or community event

Visit Joe's website at www.TILL360.com

"Bottom line . . . if you're looking for a speaker to engage, motivate, and genuinely connect with your crowd, Joe's your guy. This is the highest recommendation I can give." —**Jennifer Tiller, Chief Academic Officer, EducationPlus**

"Joe's great in front of kids, and he's even better in front of educators. Every time I go to his presentations I leave inspired." —**Hal Urban, Author, Life's Greatest Lessons**